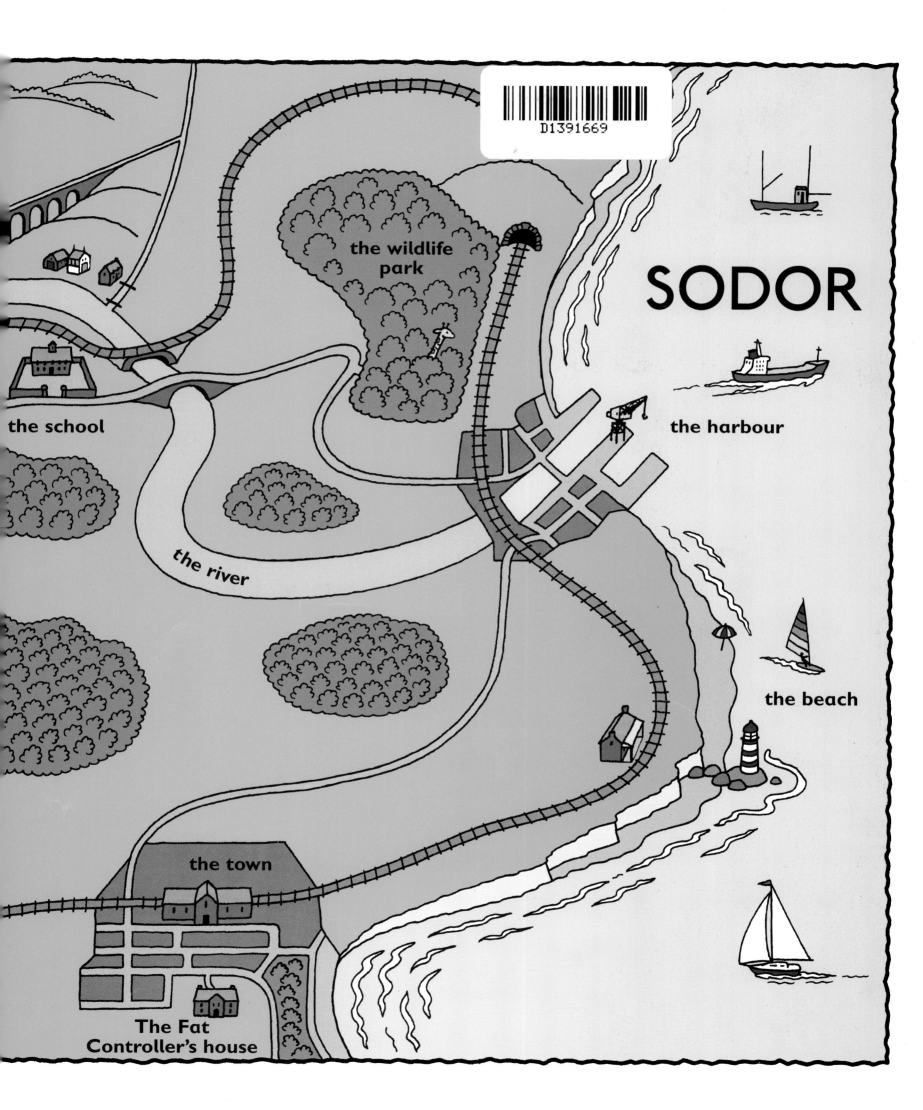

SODOR

the wildlife park

the school

the river

the harbour

the beach

the town

The Fat Controller's house

D1391669

First published in Great Britain in 1999
by Egmont Children's Books
239 Kensington High Street, London W8 6SA
Based on The Railway Series by The Rev W Awdry
Cover and line illustrations by Robin Davies
Coloured by Phil Powell & Robin Davies
Devised by Charlie Gardner and Phil Powell

THE BRITT ALLCROFT COMPANY

Britt Allcroft's Thomas the Tank Engine and Friends
Based on The Railway Series by The Rev W Awdry
© Britt Allcroft (Thomas) LLC 1999
THOMAS THE TANK ENGINE AND FRIENDS is a trademark of
Britt Allcroft Inc in the USA, Mexico and Canada and of
Britt Allcroft (Thomas) Limited in the rest of the world
THE BRITT ALLCROFT COMPANY is a trademark of
The Britt Allcroft Company plc

1 3 5 7 9 10 8 6 4 2

ISBN 0434 80465 7

Printed in Belgium

THOMAS'
Really Useful
WORD BOOK

Based on The Railway Series by The Rev. W. Awdry

red bag

teddy bear

pink bucket
and spade

suitcase

litter bin

ON THE PLATFORM

newspaper
kiosk

buffet

Snacks/Drinks

OPEN

bench

station
master

parcels

FRAGILE

buggy

coal

driver

white line

guard

platform

The Fat
Controller

porter

waiting room

clock

ticket office

TO PLATFORMS
2, 3 and 4

passenger

carriage

family

luggage
trolley

trunk

THIS WAY UP

brown briefcase

green flag

yellow umbrella

blue parcel

pigeon

IN THE COUNTRY

forest

corn field

Bertie

farm

grass

country lane

kestrel

cows

tunnel

badger

hedge

fox

mountain biker

sheep

Clarabe

rabbits

bird's nest

workmen

track

piglet

thrush

lamb

bull

cockerel

ON THE FARM

Terence

farm house

pigsty

stable

cat

boots

ax

milk churn

farmer

horse

straw bale

goat

cattle grid

hedgehog

aystack

barn

ewe

ram

hen house

barrel

log

chicken

farm truck

pond

ducks

Trevor

cows

calf

robin

sheepdog

donkey

chicks

sparrow

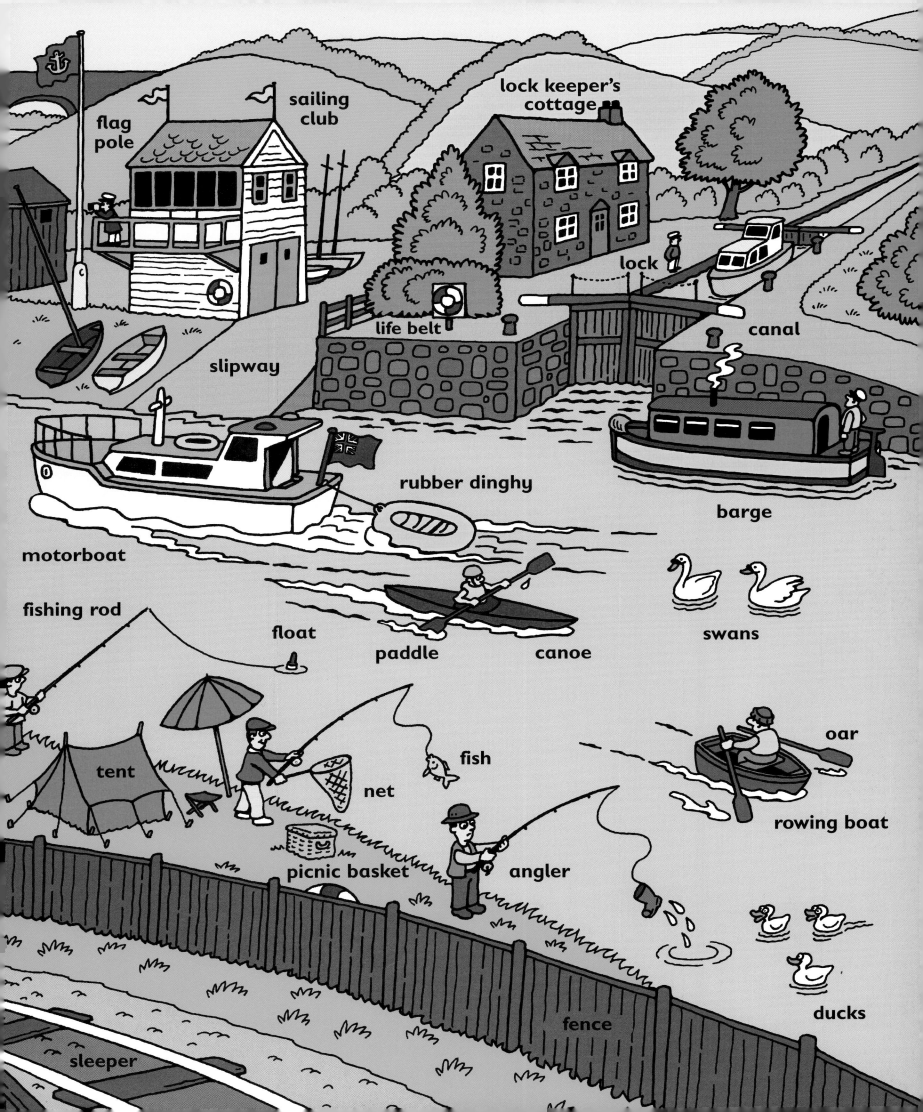

flag pole

sailing club

lock keeper's cottage

lock

canal

life belt

slipway

barge

rubber dinghy

motorboat

swans

fishing rod

float

paddle

canoe

oar

fish

tent

net

rowing boat

picnic basket

angler

fence

ducks

sleeper

hamster

crayons

dinosaur

pirate hat

Thomas book

AT SCHOOL

blackboard

globe

paint brushes

paintings

Spring

computer

teacher

chalk

register

desk

drum

books

fish tank

toy car

tambourine

fish food

recorder

Summer

Autumn

Winter

play house

window

doll

cupboard

blocks

train set

table

chair

jigsaw

mask

crown

cowboy hat

dressing-up box

aeroplane

pen

jigsaw piece

goldfish

apple

IN THE WILDLIFE PARK

crab

capstan winch

dolphin

mop

flatfish

AT THE HARBOUR

beach

crane

buoy

container

ladder

bow

container ship

diver

fish market

fishing net

rope

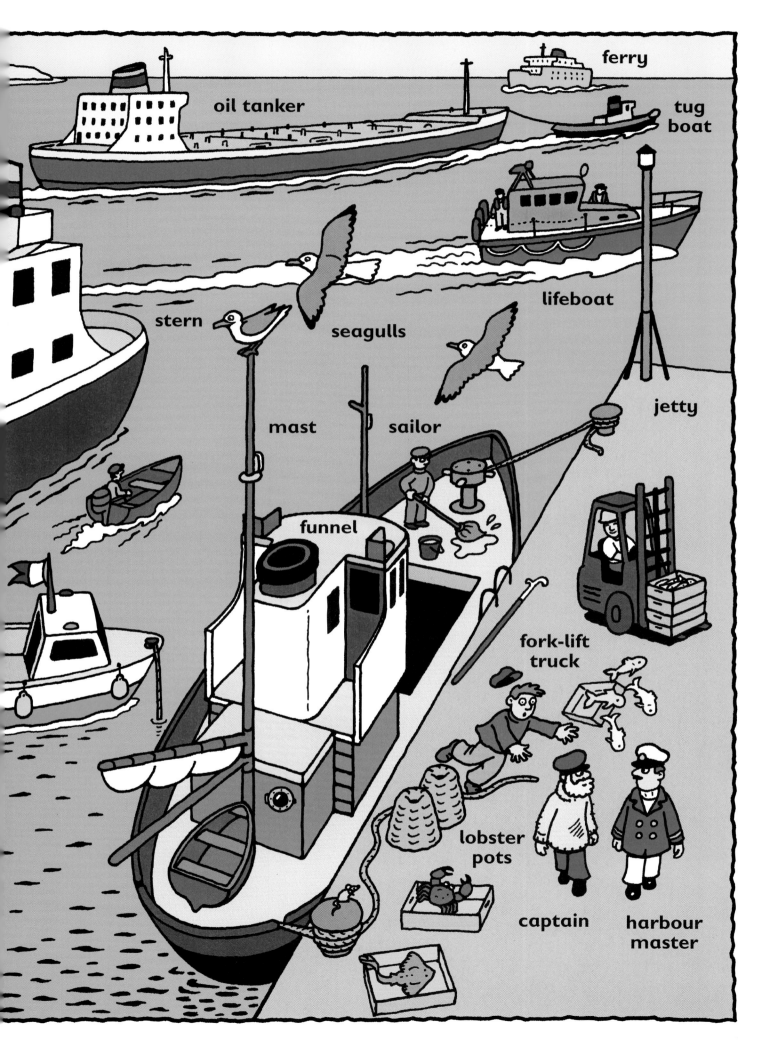

ferry

oil tanker

tug boat

lifeboat

stern

seagulls

jetty

mast

sailor

funnel

fork-lift truck

lobster pots

captain

harbour master

life belt

anchor

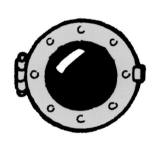

porthole

flag

lobster

sun

cliff

cafe

OPEN

steps

ice cream van

beach umbrella

deck chair

sunhat

children

puppet show

bucket

beach towel

sand castle

sunglasses

suntan lotion

spade

policeman

telephone box

motorbike

washing line

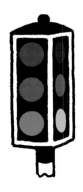

traffic lights

· IN THE TOWN ·

factory

park

playground

petrol station

carwash

statue

cinema

SQUINT & CO.

Mr. Bun

lorry

FOOT and

Annie

1

platform

steeple

house

town hall

driveway

church

fire engine

car

van

shops

coach

Dan D. Lion & Son

Eat CHEESE

TOYS B US

road

street light

police car

pavement

truck

petrol pump

aerial

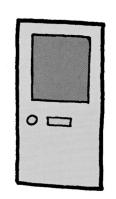

door

swings

pair of glasses

BATHROOM

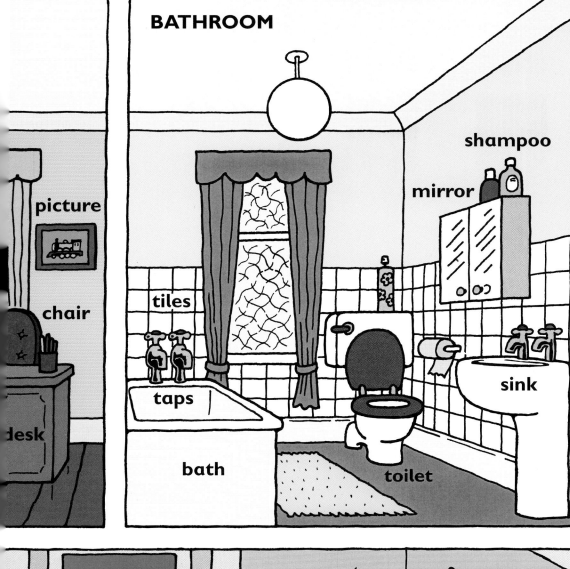

picture

chair

desk

tiles

taps

bath

shampoo

mirror

toilet

sink

BEDROOM

Harold

poster

blind

toy box

toys

letter box

front door

coat stand

mirror

telephone

floor tiles

vase

cushion

sofa

carpet

vacuum cleaner

LIVING ROOM

I am 5

badge

party hat

bow

birthday present

pink shoes

THE BIRTHDAY PARTY

juggling balls

birthday cake

clown

patio

plant pot

unicycle

steps

grass

dog

flower bed

lemonade

fairy cakes

jelly

sausage rolls

glass

jug

biscuits

cheese

table cloth

presents

table

socks

children

bouncy castle

shoes

balloons

plates

bowls

party game

blanket

spoons

blue balloon

orange juice

crisps

candles

trumpet

the station

the farm